HOW TO SURVIVE ANYTHING!

SCHOLASTIC INC.

NEW YORK • TORONTO • LONDON • AUCKLAND
YDNEY • MEXICO CITY • NEW DELHI • HONG KONG

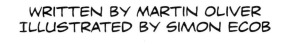

WRITTEN BY MARTIN OLIVER
ILLUSTRATED BY SIMON ECOB

EDITED BY HANNAH COHEN

DESIGNED BY ZOE QUAYLE

DISCLAIMER
The publisher and author disclaim, as far as is legally permissible,
all liability for accidents, injuries, or loss that may occur as a result
of information or instructions given in this book. Use your best common
sense at all times – particularly when using heat or sharp objects – always
wear appropriate safety gear, stay within the law and local rules, and be
considerate of other people. Always remember to ask a responsible
adult for assistance and take their advice whenever necessary.

ISBN 978-0-545-43096-8
First published in Great Britain in 2011 by Buster Books, an imprint of Michael O'Mara Books Limited.
Copyright © Buster Books 2012
Cover design by Paul Banks
All rights reserved. Published by Scholastic Inc., 557 Broadway, New York, NY 10012, by arrangement
with Buster Books. SCHOLASTIC and associated logos are trademarks and/or registered trademarks
of Scholastic Inc.

10 9 8 7 6 5 4 3 2 1   12 13 14 15 16

Printed in the USA
First American edition, May 2012

CONTENTS

WARNING!

NOT READING THIS BOOK COULD BE SERIOUSLY BAD FOR YOUR HEALTH.

HOW WOULD YOU DEAL IF THE BOAT YOU WERE ON SUDDENLY STARTED SINKING? OR IF YOU CAME FACE-TO-FACE WITH AN ANGRY CROCODILE, OR SPOTTED AN AVALANCHE OF SNOW HURTLING TOWARD YOU?

WHEN ONE FALSE MOVE COULD PROVE DISASTROUS, THERE'S ONE TOOL THAT COULD TURN OUT TO BE A LIFESAVER ... THIS BOOK! READING IT MIGHT JUST BE THE SMARTEST DECISION YOU'VE EVER MADE.

FOLLOW THE ADVICE AND ADVENTURES OF THE BOYS ON THESE PAGES AS THEY FIND THEMSELVES IN A TON OF DANGEROUS AND DEADLY SITUATIONS.

MAKE SURE YOU ARE PROPERLY PREPARED TO FACE WHATEVER THE WILDERNESS AND THE UNEXPECTED MAY THROW AT YOU!

ARE YOU READY?

YOU'LL STILL NEED ALL YOUR SKILLS, RESOURCEFULNESS, AND BRAVERY, BUT HAVING THE RIGHT INFO WILL GIVE YOU A HEAD START IN YOUR ATTEMPT TO STAY ALIVE.

POCKET PACK

WHEREVER YOU ARE, INCREASE YOUR CHANCE OF SURVIVAL BY ALWAYS CARRYING A FEW ESSENTIALS IN A SMALL CASE.

POCKET PACK ESSENTIALS:

- A MIRROR FOR SIGNALING
- A NEEDLE AND THREAD
- A FISHHOOK AND LINE
- A COMPASS • A SMALL FIRST-AID KIT, INCLUDING BANDAGES AND INSECT REPELLANT

THE BEST POCKET PACKS ARE SMALL, LIGHTWEIGHT, AND WATERPROOF.

SURVIVAL BACKPACK

IF YOU'RE ABLE TO PREPARE FOR AN EXPEDITION IN ADVANCE, CHOOSE A STURDY, WATERPROOF BACKPACK WITH POCKETS THAT SEAL, AND PACK THE EXTRA ITEMS ON THE LIST BELOW:

SURVIVAL BACKPACK ESSENTIALS:

- FUEL • A FLASHLIGHT • FOOD • A KNIFE
- ROPE OR STRING • SUNSCREEN
- A COMPLETE FIRST-AID KIT • WATER-PURIFYING TABLETS • A SLEEPING BAG/SURVIVAL BLANKET • A WATERPROOF RADIO
- SIGNALING EQUIPMENT, SUCH AS FLARES
- A CHANGE OF CLOTHING • A PLASTIC BAG

NOW TURN THE PAGE AND DISCOVER HOW TO SURVIVE ALMOST ANYTHING!

HOW TO SURVIVE A SHARK ATTACK

SHARK ATTACKS ARE RARE, BUT IF YOU DO HAPPEN TO FIND YOURSELF IN SHARK-INFESTED WATERS, STICK TO THIS ADVICE.

KEEP CLOSE TO OTHER SWIMMERS - SHARKS ARE LESS LIKELY TO ATTACK MORE THAN ONE PERSON.

IF YOU SPOT A SHARK FIN ABOVE THE WATER, SWIM BACK TO THE BEACH AS SMOOTHLY AS POSSIBLE.

SHARK! SHARK!

STOP SPLASHING AROUND - IT WILL THINK YOU'RE A FISH!

IF YOU'RE WEARING SHINY ITEMS, DITCH THEM - THESE CAN LOOK LIKE FISH SCALES TO A SHARK.

BLOOD ATTRACTS SHARKS. SO DON'T SWIM WITH GRAZES OR OPEN WOUNDS AND BE CAREFUL NOT TO CUT YOURSELF IN OPEN WATER.

THAT RING IS GONNA HAVE TO GO.

UH-OH ...

HOW TO SURVIVE FROSTBITE

WHEN YOU'RE OUT IN THE COLD, IT ISN'T JUST WILD ANIMALS AND DANGEROUS TERRAIN YOU HAVE TO LOOK OUT FOR – FROSTBITE COULD BE YOUR NUMBER-ONE ENEMY.

WHAT IS FROSTBITE?

FROSTBITE IS WHEN YOUR SKIN AND FLESH LITERALLY FREEZE.

IT ATTACKS AREAS WITH THE LEAST BLOOD CIRCULATION – YOUR HANDS, FACE, AND TOES.

UH, WHAT ARE YOU DOING?!?

I'M MOVING MY FACE TO KEEP THE CIRCULATION GOING.

WATCH OUT FOR THE WARNING SIGNS OF FROSTBITE – FIRST, THE SKIN GOES RED AND PRICKLY, THEN WAXY-LOOKING PATCHES OF GRAY SKIN WILL FORM.

THAT DOESN'T LOOK GOOD ...

IF FROSTBITE STRIKES IN YOUR HANDS, REMOVE WET GLOVES, THEN WARM YOUR HANDS UNDER YOUR ARMPITS.

BE WARNED – THAWING FROSTBITE IS PAINFUL!

IF FROSTBITE STARTS ATTACKING YOUR FEET, WARM THEM AGAINST ANOTHER PERSON'S STOMACH IF YOU CAN.

AHH, THAT'S BETTER.

UGH! THEY STINK!

DRY OUT WET CLOTHES, THEN PUT THEM BACK ON THE FROSTBITTEN AREA TO WARM IT UP.

IF THE AREA STARTS TO SWELL AND BECOMES PAINFUL, YOU NEED TO THAW IT IN WARM WATER.

CHECK THAT THE WATER ISN'T TOO HOT FIRST BY DIPPING AN ELBOW IN.

IN THE LAST STAGE OF FROSTBITE, THE SKIN BLISTERS AND BLACKENS, AND THE AFFECTED PART OF THE BODY DIES AND DROPS OFF.

LOOKS LIKE WE CAUGHT IT IN TIME.

HOW TO SURVIVE A PLANE CRASH

PLANE CRASHES ARE RARE, BUT IF YOU DO FIND YOURSELF IN A FALLING AIRCRAFT, THERE'S A LOT YOU CAN DO TO MAKE SURE YOU GET OUT OF IT ALIVE. READ ON TO FIND OUT MORE.

BEFORE TAKEOFF ...

... LISTEN TO THE SAFETY ANNOUNCEMENTS, THEN COUNT THE ROWS BETWEEN YOU AND THE NEAREST EXITS – IN A CRASH SITUATION, YOU MIGHT BE FEELING YOUR WAY OUT OF THE PLANE IN THE DARK.

... FASTEN YOUR SEAT BELT AS TIGHT AS IT WILL GO TO AVOID BEING THROWN FORWARD IF THE PLANE CRASHES.

... PRACTICE THE "BRACE POSITION" – IT'S THE SAFEST POSITION TO BE IN ON IMPACT. CUSHION YOUR HEAD ON THE SEAT IN FRONT OR REST YOUR HEAD ON YOUR KNEES AND HOLD YOUR LEGS IF THERE ISN'T A SEAT IN FRONT OF YOU.

... REMOVE ANY SHARP ITEMS FROM YOUR POCKETS, AND REMOVE GLASSES IF YOU WEAR THEM.

ONCE OUTSIDE, MOVE AWAY FROM THE PLANE - THERE MAY STILL BE DANGER FROM FIRE.

HELP ANY INJURED PEOPLE.

ARE YOU OK?

WHEN YOU'RE SURE THERE'S NO CHANCE OF A FIRE OR EXPLOSION, EXPLORE THE WRECKAGE FOR USEFUL SURVIVAL ITEMS, SUCH AS FOOD AND SHELTER EQUIPMENT.

HELP RESCUERS FIND YOU BY REMAINING NEAR THE CRASH SITE - IT SHOULD BE EASILY VISIBLE FROM THE AIR - AND SET UP DISTRESS SIGNALS, TOO.

WE NEED THREE FIRES SET UP IN A TRIANGLE - THIS IS THE INTERNATIONAL SIGN FOR BEING IN TROUBLE. AND KEEP TRYING FOR A SIGNAL ON YOUR PHONES!

USE PIECES OF WRECKAGE OR CLOTHING TO MAKE AN "X" AND A TRIANGLE SHAPE ON THE GROUND. RESCUERS KNOW THAT "X" MEANS MEDICAL ASSISTANCE NEEDED. A TRIANGLE TELLS THEM IT SHOULD BE SAFE TO LAND.

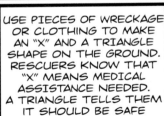

GREAT WORK, GUYS!

I'VE SPOTTED THEM.

HOW TO SURVIVE IN THE DESERT

IF YOU'RE LOST IN THE DESERT, THE FIRST THING TO DO IS FIND SHELTER FROM THE SUN.

LOOK FOR SHADOWS CAST BY TREES, BUSHES, OR ROCKS AND STAY THERE DURING THE HEAT OF THE DAY.

WHEN NIGHT FALLS, MAKE A SHELTER BY DRAPING MATERIAL OVER A LARGE ROCK OR TREE BRANCH. PILE SMALLER ROCKS AROUND THE EDGES TO KEEP THE WIND OUT.

YOUR BIGGEST PROBLEM IS LACK OF WATER – WITHOUT IT, YOU WILL LAST ONLY TWO AND A HALF DAYS....

CREATE YOUR OWN SOURCE OF WATER BY MAKING AN EMERGENCY SOLAR STILL. HERE'S HOW:

I. DIG A DEEP HOLE AND PLACE A CUP IN THE MIDDLE OF IT.

2. SURROUND THE OUTSIDE OF THE CUP WITH SPONGY PLANTS – SOFT CACTUS WORKS WELL.

3. CUT A PLASTIC BAG ALONG ONE SEAM AND ALONG THE BOTTOM EDGE TO MAKE A PLASTIC SHEET.

4. COVER THE HOLE WITH THE PLASTIC SHEET. SECURE THE SHEET USING ROCKS. PLACE A STONE IN THE MIDDLE OF IT, DIRECTLY ABOVE THE CUP.

5. THROUGHOUT THE DAY, WATER VAPOR WILL DRIP INTO THE CUP - ENOUGH FOR A SMALL DRINK, BUT NOT ENOUGH WATER TO KEEP YOU ALIVE FOR LONG.

CONSERVE BODY FLUIDS BY KEEPING YOUR MOVEMENTS SLOW AND REGULAR TO PREVENT SWEATING.

TRAVEL DURING THE NIGHT, WHEN IT IS MUCH COOLER, TO FIND OTHER SOURCES OF WATER.

HOW TO AVOID A POLAR BEAR ATTACK

IF YOU'RE TREKKING IN BEAR COUNTRY, YOU'LL NEED TO STICK TO THESE RULES TO AVOID BECOMING BEAR BRUNCH!

AVOID ATTRACTING THE ATTENTION OF A POLAR BEAR BY KEEPING A CLEAN CAMP - BEARS CAN SNIFF FOOD SMELLS FROM A LONG WAY AWAY.

STAY AWAY FROM MAMMAL CARCASSES. POLAR BEARS ARE SCAVENGERS AND WILL BE ATTRACTED TO THE PROSPECT OF A FREE MEAL.

NEVER PET A POLAR BEAR CUB - ITS MOTHER WON'T LIKE IT AND SHE MAY BE HIDING JUST AROUND THE CORNER!

IF YOU'RE UNLUCKY ENOUGH TO BE APPROACHED BY A POLAR BEAR, STAND YOUR GROUND. IT MAY THINK YOU LOOK LIKE TOO MUCH TROUBLE TO ATTACK COMPARED TO A TEENY, TINY SEAL.

MAKE YOURSELF LOOK AS BIG AND SCARY AS POSSIBLE BY STANDING TALL AND HOLDING A JACKET OVER YOUR HEAD.

IF THIS DOESN'T WORK, SHOUT LOUDLY AT THE BEAR TO SCARE IT OFF.

AAH!

WHATEVER YOU DO, DON'T RUN AWAY – A BEAR WILL ALWAYS OUTRUN YOU!

HOW TO SURVIVE A FLASH FLOOD

HOW TO SURVIVE A BROKEN LEG

AFTER AN ACCIDENT, YOU MAY FIND ONE OF YOUR TEAM IS FACED WITH AN INJURY, SUCH AS A BROKEN LEG. HOW WOULD YOU TREAT IT? READ ON TO FIND OUT.

LOOK AT THE WOUND – PAIN, TENDERNESS, AND SWELLING ARE ALL SIGNS OF A BROKEN LEG. DO NOT MOVE IT. SEEK MEDICAL ATTENTION IMMEDIATELY.

OW, IT HURTS!

IF YOU ARE STUCK OUT IN THE WILD, FOLLOW THESE STEPS:

IF THE SKIN IS BROKEN, DON'T PUT ANYTHING ON THE WOUND. IF IT'S BLEEDING HEAVILY, HOWEVER, APPLY STEADY PRESSURE USING A STERILE BANDAGE TO STOP THE FLOW.

IT'S OK, YOU'RE NOT BLEEDING.

MAKE A SPLINT – THIS "SETS" THE LIMB SO THAT THE BROKEN BONES STAY IN PLACE. FIRST, FIND TWO PIECES OF SIMILAR-SIZED WOOD.

HOW TO SURVIVE AN EARTHQUAKE

EARTHQUAKES OCCUR WHEN ROCKS IN EARTH'S CRUST MOVE SUDDENLY, CAUSING THE GROUND ABOVE TO SHAKE. THE EFFECTS CAN BE DEVASTATING. FOLLOW THIS ADVICE TO MAKE SURE YOU SURVIVE IF ONE STRIKES.

IF YOU'RE IN AN EARTHQUAKE ZONE, LISTEN FOR WARNING REPORTS.

IF YOU HAVE ANY ADVANCE WARNING OF AN EARTHQUAKE COMING, TURN OFF COOKING APPLIANCES AND GAS AND ELECTRICITY LINES – THEY COULD RUPTURE AND CAUSE A FIRE DURING A QUAKE.

IF A QUAKE STRIKES ...

... STAY INDOORS! KEEP AWAY FROM LARGE OBJECTS THAT COULD FALL ON YOU, AND FIND A STURDY PIECE OF FURNITURE TO SHELTER BENEATH.

STAY AWAY FROM WINDOWS THAT MIGHT SHATTER NEAR YOU.

IF YOU'RE NOT NEAR A PIECE OF FURNITURE, CROUCH IN AN INSIDE CORNER OF A BUILDING AND COVER YOUR FACE AND HEAD WITH YOUR HANDS.

IF YOU'RE IN BED WHEN IT STRIKES AND THERE'S NOTHING ON THE CEILING ABOVE YOU, STAY THERE AND COVER YOUR HEAD WITH A PILLOW.

BEWARE OF AFTERSHOCKS, WHICH CAN BE AS DESTRUCTIVE AS THE ORIGINAL QUAKE.

WAIT UNTIL THE TREMORS HAVE STOPPED BEFORE LEAVING YOUR SHELTER, AND ONLY MEET OTHER SURVIVORS IN OPEN SPACES, AWAY FROM FALLING DEBRIS OR DAMAGED BUILDINGS.

BECOME AN EARTHQUAKE EXPERT!

THE STRENGTH OF EARTHQUAKES IS MEASURED ON A SCALE CALLED A "RICHTER SCALE."

LESS THAN 1.0 – 2.9: NOT NOTICEABLE NORMALLY BUT MEASURABLE
3.0 – 3.9: EARTHQUAKE FELT BUT DAMAGE RARE
4.0 – 4.9: WIDELY FELT WITH SOME LOCAL BUT NOT SIGNIFICANT DAMAGE
5.0 – 5.9: DAMAGE TO POORLY CONSTRUCTED BUILDINGS
6.0 – 6.9: DAMAGE IN BUILT-UP AREAS
7.0 – 7.9: MAJOR QUAKE WITH DAMAGE OVER LARGE AREAS
8.0 AND HIGHER: WIDESPREAD DESTRUCTION WITH FATAL CONSEQUENCES

HOW TO SURVIVE A FOREST FIRE

FOREST FIRES ARE UNPREDICTABLE AND CAN EXPLODE WITH ALMOST NO WARNING. FOLLOW THESE RULES AND BE READY IF ONE STRIKES.

IF YOU'RE STAYING IN AN AREA AT RISK, KEEP AN EYE ON LOCAL NEWS FOR FIRE WARNINGS.

IF A FIRE IS REPORTED, CLEAR VEGETATION AND ANY FLAMMABLE MATERIALS WITHIN 12 YARDS OF YOUR HOUSE. SOAK THE GROUND WITH WATER, TOO.

TURN OFF ALL GAS SUPPLIES. THEN PLAN AN EXIT ROUTE — TRAVEL LIGHT AND FAST.

IF YOU NEED TO EVACUATE, PUT ON LONG SLEEVES AND PANTS. SOAK A BLANKET IN WATER AND PLACE A WET HANDKERCHIEF OVER YOUR MOUTH.

HOW TO SURVIVE IN A WHITEOUT

DURING A SNOW BLIZZARD, VISIBILITY CAN BECOME SO BAD THAT PEOPLE BECOME LOST AND DISORIENTED. THIS IS CALLED A WHITEOUT. FOLLOW THIS ADVICE IF ONE STRIKES.

WATCH OUT FOR LOOMING, LOW, DARK CLOUDS, AND AN INCREASE IN THE WIND - THESE ARE SIGNS OF A BLIZZARD APPROACHING.

IF A BLIZZARD BEGINS, HEAD FOR SHELTER - BOULDERS, CAVES, OR TREES.

IF A WHITEOUT OCCURS, REMAIN WHERE YOU ARE - YOU COULD GET LOST OR FALL INTO RAVINES HIDDEN BY THE SNOW.

TURN YOUR BACK TO THE WIND AND COVER YOUR MOUTH, NOSE, AND EYES TO KEEP FREEZING AIR OUT.

HOW TO SURVIVE A ZOMBIE INVASION

IF YOUR TOWN IS INVADED BY ZOMBIES – OR THE "UNDEAD," AS THEY PREFER TO BE KNOWN – YOU WILL NEED A PLAN ... FAST!

SPOTTING A ZOMBIE IS SIMPLE – THEY WALK SLOWLY AND JERKILY, DROOL SALIVA, HAVE WILD EYES, ARE OFTEN DIRTY, AND ARE COVERED IN BOILS AND OPEN WOUNDS.

ZOMBIES FEED ON LIVING FLESH AND WILL BE LOOKING FOR YOU, SO YOU WILL NEED TO MAKE A SECURE SHELTER.

A SHELTER IS THE PERFECT PLACE TO STORE FOOD AND TEAM UP WITH OTHER SURVIVORS.

UNFORTUNATELY, IT MAY EVENTUALLY ATTRACT HORDES OF ZOMBIES WHO SMELL FRESH MEAT.

KNOW YOUR EXITS. IF ZOMBIES HAVE SNIFFED YOU OUT, ABANDON YOUR SHELTER AND FIND ANOTHER.

UHH ... IT'S TIME TO MOVE ON, GUYS. LET'S LEAVE OUT THE BACK.

CHECK STRANGERS FOR CUTS OR BITES. IF A ZOMBIE BREAKS THE SKIN OF ITS VICTIMS, IT'S ONLY A MATTER OF TIME UNTIL THEY TURN INTO ZOMBIES THEMSELVES.

WHEN ON THE MOVE, STAY ALERT. CARRY SAUSAGES TO USE AS A DISTRACTION IF YOU NEED TO.

IF YOU BUMP INTO A ZOMBIE, YOU'LL PROBABLY BE ABLE TO OUTRUN THEM - THEY ARE PRETTY SLOW.

WEAR GLOVES AND BODY ARMOR TO PROTECT AGAINST ZOMBIE BITES AND SCRATCHES.

IF YOU'RE AMBUSHED OR CAN'T ESCAPE ... USE A BIT OF BRAIN POWER!

ADOPT A ZOMBIE POSE AND SHUFFLE SLOWLY.

RIP YOUR CLOTHES AND SMEAR DIRT OVER YOUR SKIN.

DROOL AND ROAR, THEN WANDER OFF WHEN NO ONE'S LOOKING.

ZOMBIES ARE HARD TO BATTLE BECAUSE THEY ARE ALREADY TECHNICALLY DEAD. SHOOTING THEM OR HACKING OFF A LIMB WILL ONLY SLOW THEM DOWN. INSTEAD, HIT THEM AS HARD AS YOU CAN ON THEIR HEAD - THIS SHOULD FINISH THEM OFF.

HOW TO SURVIVE A SNAKEBITE

WASH AWAY ANY VENOM LEFT ON THE SKIN WITH WATER AND SOAP IF POSSIBLE.

SLOWING THE FLOW OF BLOOD THROUGH THE BODY SLOWS THE MOVEMENT OF VENOM AND CAN BUY YOU VITAL EXTRA HOURS TO GET TREATMENT.

TO DO THIS, FIRST WRAP A SINGLE BANDAGE ABOVE THE BITE, AND THEN OVER THE BITE ITSELF. BE CAREFUL NOT TO WRAP THE BANDAGE TOO TIGHTLY.

NEVER CUT THE FLESH AROUND THE BITE AND SUCK OUT THE VENOM LIKE YOU SEE IN THE MOVIES. THIS MAY ONLY HELP TO SPREAD THE VENOM AND CAUSE INFECTION.

STAY STILL AND RELAX.

DO EVERYTHING YOU CAN TO CONTACT EMERGENCY MEDICAL SERVICES, AND KEEP THE VICTIM AS STILL AND CALM AS POSSIBLE. THIS WILL HELP SLOW THE MOVEMENT OF VENOM THROUGH THE BODY UNTIL HELP ARRIVES.

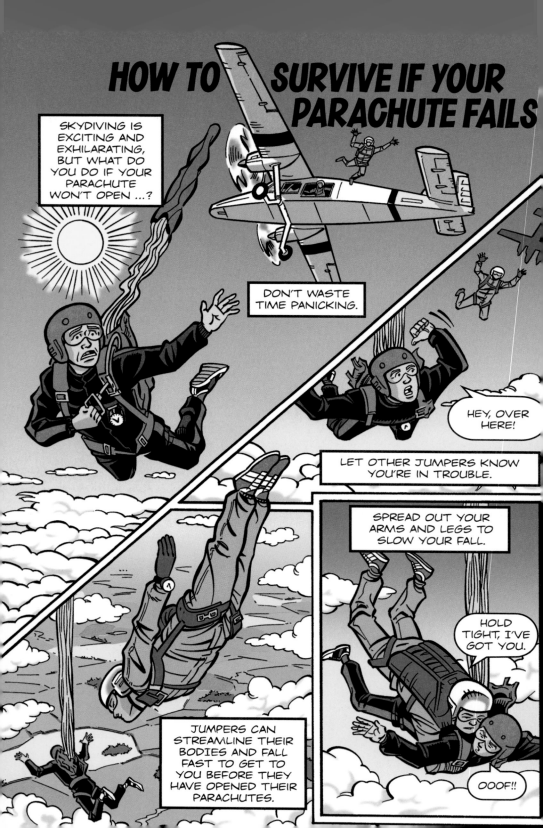

GET A GOOD GRIP ON YOUR COMPANION, SO THAT WHEN HIS PARACHUTE OPENS AND HE STARTS TO FALL MORE SLOWLY, THE FORCE OF IT DOESN'T PULL YOU OFF.

BRACE YOURSELF. THE FORCE OF A PARACHUTE OPENING WITH YOUR COMBINED WEIGHTS COULD DISLOCATE YOUR SHOULDERS OR BREAK YOUR ARMS.

HOLD ON TIGHT TO MY SHOULDER STRAPS, I'M OPENING MY PARACHUTE ... NOW!

ONCE THE CANOPY OF THE PARACHUTE IS OPEN, TRY TO LAND IN WATER. AFTER LANDING, QUICKLY HELP EACH OTHER TO SHORE BEFORE YOUR PARACHUTES FILL WITH WATER AND GET TOO HEAVY TO LIFT.

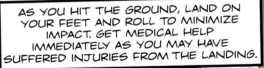

IF THERE IS NO WATER AROUND, LOOK FOR A FIELD TO LAND ON INSTEAD.

AS YOU HIT THE GROUND, LAND ON YOUR FEET AND ROLL TO MINIMIZE IMPACT. GET MEDICAL HELP IMMEDIATELY AS YOU MAY HAVE SUFFERED INJURIES FROM THE LANDING.

I CAN SEE ONE. IT'S GOING TO BE A ROUGH LANDING!

HANG ON, BUDDY, ALMOST THERE ...

HOW TO SURVIVE A CROC ATTACK

CROCODILES ARE SERIOUS PREDATORS. THEY CAN LIVE IN SALT WATER OR FRESHWATER AND CAN GROW UP TO OVER 20 FEET LONG. TO SURVIVE AN ATTACK, KNOW AS MUCH AS POSSIBLE ABOUT THEM.

FACT
CROCODILES ARE MOST ACTIVE AT MORNING AND AT DUSK.

FACT
ONLY THEIR EYES, EARS, AND NOSTRILS CAN BE SEEN FROM ABOVE THE SURFACE OF THE WATER.

FACT
THEY RUN QUICKLY (UP TO 17 MILES AN HOUR), BUT ONLY FOR SHORT DISTANCES.

FACT
THEIR SKIN IS COVERED IN HARD, BONY PLATES.

FACT
DESPITE HAVING INCREDIBLY POWERFUL JAWS, CROCODILES HAVE WEAK MUSCLES FOR OPENING THEIR MOUTHS.

FACT
WEAK AREAS ON THEIR BODIES INCLUDE THE EYES, NOSTRILS, AND EARS.

FACT
SECRET WEAK SPOT: THE PALATAL VALVE. IT'S A FLAP JUST BEHIND THE TONGUE THAT COVERS A CROCODILE'S THROAT WHEN SUBMERGED SO IT DOESN'T DROWN UNDERWATER.

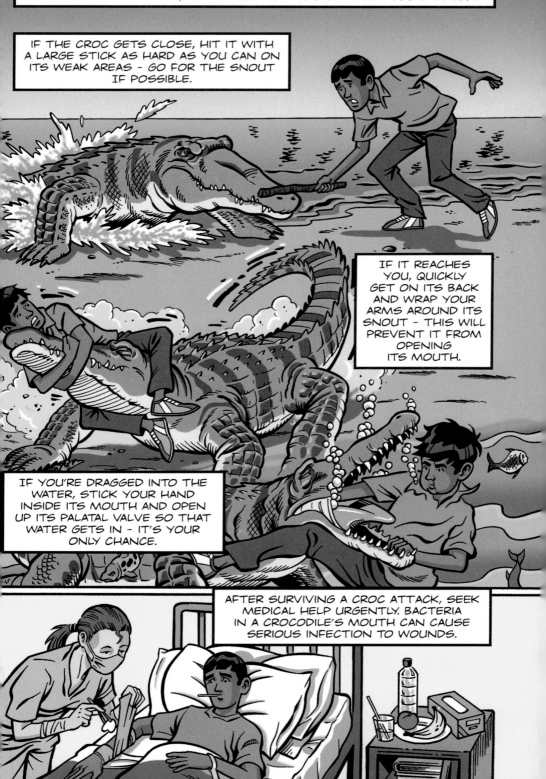

IF YOU'RE STUCK OUT IN THE OPEN, STAY THERE, BUT DON'T ...

... GO NEAR TOWERS ...

... OR OPEN AN UMBRELLA – ESPECIALLY IF IT HAS A METAL SPIKE ...

... OR TAKE SHELTER UNDER TALL TREES, WHICH ARE MORE LIKELY TO GET STRUCK.

INSTEAD, GET INTO THE LIGHTNING-SAFETY CROUCH TO STAY ALIVE:

FIRST, TAKE OFF YOUR WATCH AND ANY OTHER METAL ITEMS. THROW THEM FAR AWAY FROM YOU.

NEXT, CROUCH DOWN AND COVER YOUR EARS WITH YOUR HANDS TO PROTECT THEM FROM THUNDER.

STAY IN THE CROUCH POSITION UNTIL THE STORM HAS PASSED BEFORE GETTING UP AND HEADING FOR SHELTER.

STAY DOWN!!

HOW TO SURVIVE A T-REX

IMAGINE BEING ZAPPED BACK IN TIME OVER 65 MILLION YEARS AND SPOTTING A DEADLY PREHISTORIC PREDATOR - A TYRANNOSAURUS REX! FOLLOW THESE DOS AND DON'TS TO STAY ALIVE.

DO STAY ALERT - ALTHOUGH T-REXS WERE EASY TO SPOT AT UP TO 20 FEET TALL, THEY MIGHT HAVE SURPRISED PREY BY ATTACKING THEM FROM THE BUSHES.

DON'T ASSUME THERE IS ONLY ONE EITHER ... T-REXS MAY HAVE HUNTED LARGER PREY IN PACKS.

DON'T STAY PUT AND PLAY DEAD - T-REXS HAD AN EXCELLENT SENSE OF SMELL SO THEY COULD EASILY SNIFF OUT THEIR NEXT MEAL.

DON'T BE TEMPTED TO STAY AND FIGHT. EVEN THOUGH A T-REX'S ARMS WERE CONSIDERABLY SMALLER THAN ITS MASSIVE BACK LEGS, IT COULD STILL PACK A POWERFUL PUNCH.

DO RUN AWAY IN A ZIGZAG FOR AS LONG AS YOU CAN. THE T-REX HAD A HUGE TAIL AND POWERFUL BACK LEGS, WHICH MEANT IT COULD PROBABLY OUTSPRINT A HUMAN BEING OVER SHORT DISTANCES.

DON'T GET TRAMPLED ON – WEIGHING IN AT AROUND 15,000 POUNDS, A T-REX WOULD SQUASH YOU FLAT.

DO AVOID A T-REX'S JAWS. WITH OVER 60 RAZOR-SHARP TEETH, IT COULD PROBABLY GULP DOWN ABOUT 500 POUNDS OF MEAT IN ONE BITE. THAT'S WAY MORE THAN THE WHOLE OF YOU!

WHY HAS IT GONE DARK?

HOW TO SURVIVE A SINKING SHIP

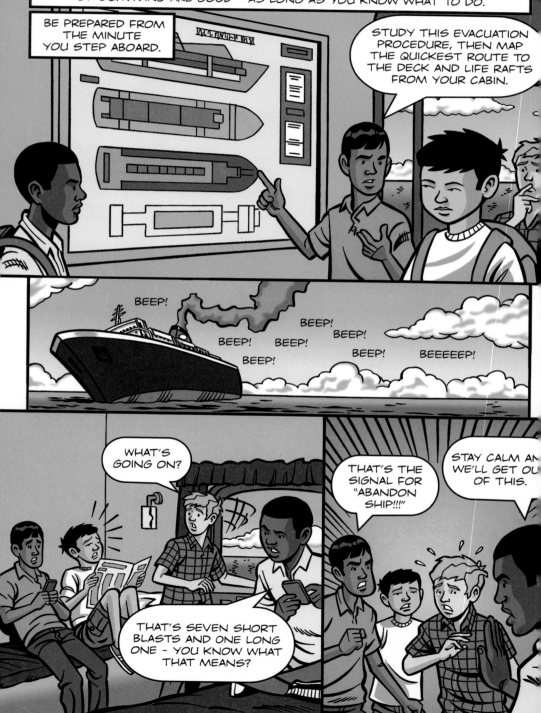

GRAB THAT BAG AND LET'S GO!

ALWAYS PREPARE AN EVACUATION BAG IN CASE YOUR SHIP SINKS AND YOU ARE STRANDED AT SEA. INCLUDE:

• A COMPASS • A FLASHLIGHT • A WATERPROOF JACKET • MATCHES • A KNIFE • SUNSCREEN LOTION • WATER • FOOD • A MIRROR FOR SIGNALING • FLARES • A FIRST-AID KIT • A FISHHOOK AND LINE

EVERYONE GET UP ON DECK AS QUICKLY AS POSSIBLE.

TRY NOT TO PANIC - THIS WILL ONLY SLOW YOUR ESCAPE DOWN.

BREATHE DEEPLY AND TRY TO RELAX. WE'LL GET OUT OF HERE ALIVE IF YOU FOLLOW ME.

PUT ON A LIFE JACKET BEFORE GETTING INTO THE LIFE RAFTS BUT DON'T INFLATE IT UNTIL YOU HAVE LEFT THE SHIP.

IF YOU FIND YOURSELF IN THE WATER WITHOUT A LIFE JACKET, MAKE A FLOAT USING YOUR PANTS BY FOLLOWING THESE STEPS:

1. TAKE YOUR PANTS OFF, THEN TIE A KNOT AT THE END OF EACH LEG.

2. SWING THEM ABOVE YOUR HEAD TO FILL THEM WITH AIR, THEN PULL DOWNWARD INTO THE WATER TO TRAP THE AIR INSIDE THEM.

3. HOLD THE PANTS AT THE WAIST AND USE THE LEGS AS A FLOAT.

HOW TO SURVIVE A VAMPIRE ATTACK

STRONG, SUPERFAST, AND BLOODTHIRSTY - YOU DON'T WANT TO WRESTLE WITH A VAMPIRE UNLESS YOU'RE PROPERLY PREPARED ...

FIRST, LEARN HOW TO SPOT ONE - THEY ARE OFTEN THIN, PALE, AND VERY WELL DRESSED.

NEXT, GATHER THE FOLLOWING TO BATTLE ONE:

A CRUCIFIX - THEY FREAK VAMPIRES OUT.

BODY ARMOR - TO MAKE YOUR SKIN FANGPROOF.

ARE YOU A VAMPIRE?

NO, I'M JUST COOL.

CLOVES OF GARLIC - VAMPIRES HATE THE STUFF!

A HOCKEY STICK - BEHEAD A VAMPIRE WITH ONE OF THESE TO KILL IT.

A SHARPENED SILVER STAKE - A STAB THROUGH A VAMPIRE'S HEART WILL KILL IT. AVOID WOODEN STAKES - ONCE THE WOOD ROTS, THE VAMPIRE CAN RETURN TO LIFE!

MATCHES AND CANDLES - VAMPIRES WILL BURN TO ASH IF SET ON FIRE.

HOLY WATER - THIS BURNS THEIR SKIN.

HOW TO SURVIVE AN AVALANCHE

 **DON'T** THINK YOU CAN OUT-SKI AN AVALANCHE - THE SNOW CAN BE TRAVELING AS FAST AS 60 MILES PER HOUR!

DO STAY AS CLOSE TO THE SURFACE OF THE SNOW AS POSSIBLE BY SWIMMING UPWARD THROUGH THE SLIDING SNOW.

MANY AVALANCHE VICTIMS ARE DROWNED BY SNOW, SO TRY TO KEEP YOUR MOUTH SHUT AT ALL TIMES. WHEN THE SNOW SETTLES, WIGGLE YOUR HEAD AND USE YOUR ARMS TO CLEAR SOME BREATHING SPACE.

TAKE A DEEP BREATH AND HOLD IT FOR A FEW SECONDS - THIS EXPANDS YOUR CHEST AND CREATES SOME EXTRA SPACE.

IF YOU CAN MOVE, TRY TO PUSH A LEG OR ARM OUT OF THE SNOW AND STAY CALM WHILE YOU WAIT FOR RESCUERS TO USE YOUR GPS TO LOCATE YOU.

HOW TO SURVIVE A TORNADO

TORNADOS ARE FUNNELS OF VIOLENT, SPINNING AIR THAT COME OUT OF THUNDERSTORMS. READ ON TO FIND OUT WHAT TO DO IF ONE HITS.

IF YOU CAN, GET INSIDE A BUILDING AND GET DOWN TO THE LOWEST LEVEL - A BASEMENT IS IDEAL.

IF THERE'S NO BASEMENT, FIND A ROOM IN THE MIDDLE OF THE BUILDING - A HALLWAY OR INSIDE BATHROOM IS PERFECT.

CROUCH UNDER A STURDY PIECE OF FURNITURE, FAR AWAY FROM ANY WINDOWS THAT MIGHT SHATTER IN THE WIND.

PROTECT YOUR HEAD WITH YOUR HANDS AND ARMS.

IF THERE'S NO STURDY FURNITURE TO HIDE UNDER, BUILD A SHELTER OUT OF MATTRESSES AND PROTECT YOUR HEAD WITH A HELMET, IF YOU CAN.

IF YOU CAN'T GET INSIDE A BUILDING IN TIME, RUN AWAY FROM TEMPORARY STRUCTURES THAT COULD BE PICKED UP BY THE TORNADO ...

... AND AVOID AREAS WITH LOTS OF TREES AND CARS. QUICKLY FIND A DITCH AND LIE DOWN FLAT UNTIL THE STORM PASSES.

IF YOU'RE IN A CAR WHEN A TORNADO STRIKES, GET OUT AND RUN TO THE CLOSEST BUILDING AS FAST AS YOU CAN.

IF THERE ARE NO BUILDINGS, DRIVE AWAY FROM THE TORNADO AT A 90-DEGREE ANGLE.

AVOID CROSSING OVER ANY BRIDGES AND DON'T PARK IN UNDERPASSES – THEY DON'T OFFER MUCH PROTECTION.

IF THE TORNADO REACHES YOU, GET OUT OF THE CAR AND LIE FLAT IN A DITCH. COVER YOUR FACE AND EYES TO PROTECT THEM FROM FLYING DEBRIS.

HOW TO SURVIVE QUICKSAND

QUICKSAND IS SAND THAT IS SATURATED WITH WATER. IT'S USUALLY ONLY 3 FEET DEEP, BUT YOUR LOWER BODY CAN GET WEDGED WITHIN IT. ONCE THAT HAPPENS, IT'S HARD TO ESCAPE. READ ON TO FIND OUT HOW TO AVOID A STICKY, SANDY END.

OK, TEAM, WALK CAREFULLY – QUICKSAND COULD BE LURKING ANYWHERE AROUND HERE.

STAY ALERT IN MARSHY COASTAL AREAS OR BEACHES WITH STRONG TIDES – THAT'S WHERE YOU'LL USUALLY ENCOUNTER DANGEROUS QUICKSAND.

USE A LONG STICK TO PROD THE GROUND IN FRONT OF YOU – IF YOU FEEL IT GETTING STUCK, WARN OTHERS.

CAREFUL, GUYS, QUICKSAND OVER HERE!

IF YOU START SINKING, DON'T PANIC AND THRASH AROUND. THE MORE YOU MOVE, THE MORE YOU WILL SINK.

I THINK I FOUND SOME MORE ...

IF YOU GET STUCK, THROW AWAY HEAVY EQUIPMENT AND LIE BACKWARD AS QUICKLY AND AS FLAT AS YOU CAN. THIS WILL STOP YOU SINKING FARTHER.

BE CAREFUL NOT TO GET DRAGGED IN TOO, GUYS!

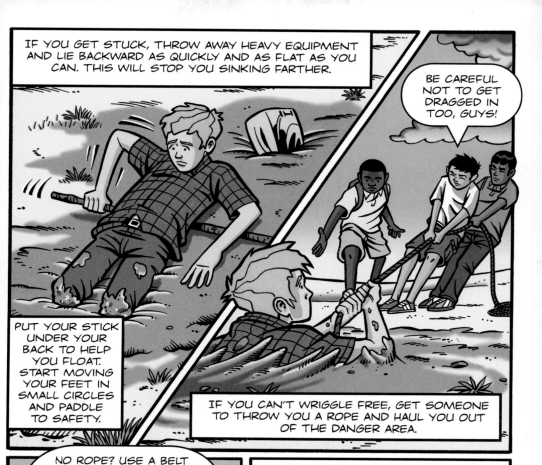

PUT YOUR STICK UNDER YOUR BACK TO HELP YOU FLOAT. START MOVING YOUR FEET IN SMALL CIRCLES AND PADDLE TO SAFETY.

IF YOU CAN'T WRIGGLE FREE, GET SOMEONE TO THROW YOU A ROPE AND HAUL YOU OUT OF THE DANGER AREA.

NO ROPE? USE A BELT INSTEAD, OR UNCLIP THE STRAPS FROM YOUR BACKPACK AND TIE THEM TOGETHER TO MAKE ONE.

IF YOU'RE TOTALLY STUCK, DIG AROUND YOUR BODY TO RELIEVE THE SUCTION. ADD WATER TO MAKE THE SAND THINNER AND EASIER TO MOVE AROUND IN, UNTIL YOU ARE ABLE TO FLOAT TO FREEDOM.

HOW TO SURVIVE A FALL

IF YOU'RE EVER FORCED TO MAKE A JUMP FOR SAFETY, CHECK OUT THIS GUIDE TO HELP INCREASE YOUR CHANCES OF SURVIVAL.

FAST-FLOWING WATER IS THE BEST THING YOU CAN LAND ON IF YOU HAVE A CHOICE.

AIM TO LAND IN THE DEEPEST WATER - THIS IS GENERALLY IN THE MIDDLE OF A BODY OF WATER.

AFTER YOU'VE JUMPED, GET YOUR BODY INTO AN UPRIGHT POSITION AND KEEP YOUR FEET TOGETHER WHEN YOU HIT THE WATER.

AS SOON AS YOU ENTER THE WATER, SPREAD YOUR ARMS AND LEGS OUT AND MOVE THEM BACK AND FORTH - THIS WILL SLOW YOU DOWN.

AS SOON AS YOU SURFACE, SWIM TO THE SAFETY OF THE SHORE.

THAT WAS CLOSE!

HOW TO SURVIVE A SWARM OF BEES

THE GOOD NEWS ABOUT BEES ...	THE BAD NEWS ABOUT BEES ...
... IS THAT THEY GENERALLY DON'T GO CHASING AFTER PEOPLE ON PURPOSE.	... IS THAT IF YOU SEE A SWARM HEADING TOWARD YOU, YOU'RE PROBABLY NEAR THEIR HIVE.

TO SURVIVE AN ATTACK YOU WILL NEED TO MOVE AND THINK FAST.

DO COVER YOUR FACE WITH YOUR SHIRT, ESPECIALLY YOUR MOUTH AND NOSE. THIS WILL STOP THE BEES STINGING THESE SENSITIVE AREAS. IF YOU'VE GOT SUNGLASSES, PUT THEM ON.

DO HEAD INSIDE A BUILDING, A CAR, OR A TENT IF YOU ARE NEAR ONE. COVER YOURSELF WITH A BLANKET IF YOU CAN.

DO RUN AS FAST AS YOU CAN AWAY FROM THE SWARM IF YOU CAN'T GET TO SHELTER.

DON'T SWAT AT THE BEES - THEY ARE ATTRACTED TO MOVEMENT AND MORE BEES MAY FOLLOW YOU.

DON'T HEAD BACK TOWARD THE HIVE, EVEN IF YOU LEFT SOMETHING BEHIND.

DON'T DIVE INTO WATER - THE SWARM CAN HOVER ABOVE AND WILL ATTACK WHEN YOU SURFACE.

WHEN THE COAST IS CLEAR, FOLLOW THESE STEPS AS QUICKLY AS POSSIBLE:

1. IF YOU'VE BEEN STUNG MORE THAN ONCE, OR IN OR AROUND THE MOUTH OR NOSE, SEEK MEDICAL ATTENTION IMMEDIATELY.

2. REMOVE THE STINGER AS QUICKLY AS POSSIBLE.

BEE STINGERS HAVE TINY HOOKS ON THEM THAT CAN GET STUCK IN YOUR SKIN IF YOU JUST PULL THEM OUT. AVOID THIS BY SCRAPING THE EDGE OF A RULER IN A SCOOPING MOTION ACROSS THE STINGER TO REMOVE IT.

3. CLEAN THE AREA WITH WARM WATER AND SOAP.

4. APPLY ICE OR COLD WATER TO REDUCE ANY SWELLING.

SOME PEOPLE ARE ALLERGIC TO BEE STINGS. IF YOU HAVE ANY OF THE SYMPTOMS BELOW, CALL EMERGENCY MEDICAL SERVICES IMMEDIATELY.

- VOMITING, DIARRHEA, OR FEELING SICK
- DIZZINESS
- DIFFICULTY BREATHING

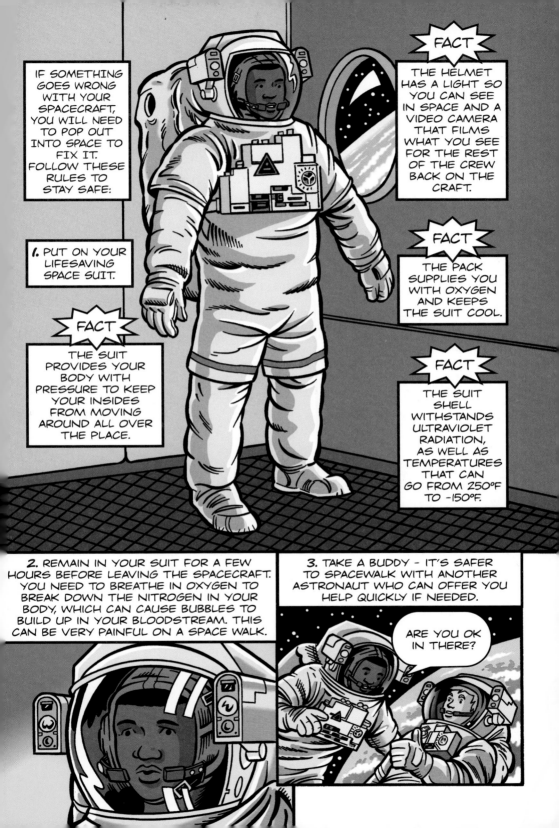

IF SOMETHING GOES WRONG WITH YOUR SPACECRAFT, YOU WILL NEED TO POP OUT INTO SPACE TO FIX IT. FOLLOW THESE RULES TO STAY SAFE:

1. PUT ON YOUR LIFESAVING SPACE SUIT.

FACT

THE SUIT PROVIDES YOUR BODY WITH PRESSURE TO KEEP YOUR INSIDES FROM MOVING AROUND ALL OVER THE PLACE.

FACT

THE HELMET HAS A LIGHT SO YOU CAN SEE IN SPACE AND A VIDEO CAMERA THAT FILMS WHAT YOU SEE FOR THE REST OF THE CREW BACK ON THE CRAFT.

FACT

THE PACK SUPPLIES YOU WITH OXYGEN AND KEEPS THE SUIT COOL.

FACT

THE SUIT SHELL WITHSTANDS ULTRAVIOLET RADIATION, AS WELL AS TEMPERATURES THAT CAN GO FROM 250°F TO -150°F.

2. REMAIN IN YOUR SUIT FOR A FEW HOURS BEFORE LEAVING THE SPACECRAFT. YOU NEED TO BREATHE IN OXYGEN TO BREAK DOWN THE NITROGEN IN YOUR BODY, WHICH CAN CAUSE BUBBLES TO BUILD UP IN YOUR BLOODSTREAM. THIS CAN BE VERY PAINFUL ON A SPACE WALK.

3. TAKE A BUDDY - IT'S SAFER TO SPACEWALK WITH ANOTHER ASTRONAUT WHO CAN OFFER YOU HELP QUICKLY IF NEEDED.

ARE YOU OK IN THERE?

ALSO AVAILABLE ...

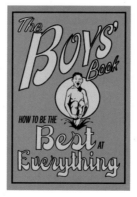

The Boys' Book: How to Be
the Best at Everything
978-0-545-01628-5

The Girls' Book: How to Be
the Best at Everything
978-0-545-01629-2

The Girls' Book of Glamour:
A Guide to Being a Goddess
978-0-545-08537-3

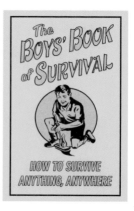

The Boys' Book of Survival:
How to Survive Anything,
Anywhere
978-0-545-08536-6

Thirty Days Has September:
Cool Ways to Remember Stuff
978-0-545-10740-2